the D-60 challenge

your journey towards mindfulness

r.ravisha

to all those who feel lost in this vast sea,
may this serve as an anchor to guide you toward the
shores of peace and mindfulness you seek.

What is the D-60 Challenge All About?

The D-60 Challenge is a collection of mindfulness activities designed to turn theory into practice. Having practiced these activities myself for over a year, I can confidently say they work. The challenge involves starting with one activity per day for 60 days and eventually transitioning to practicing a set of any five activities daily, interchangeably.

The beauty of this challenge lies in its flexibility. You can start whenever you're ready—just remember that consistency is key.

Why a Journal?

This isn't just a book—it's a journal. The format is intentional, allowing you to keep the activities and your personal entries side by side. We've all read self-help books, only to struggle with applying their tips. The D-60 Challenge bridges that gap, helping you declutter your mind, gain clarity, and equip yourself to become your most productive and mindful self. After every activity, write down your experience and reflections about that activity.

By the end of this challenge, you'll have a tangible record of your growth—a subjective graph of your journey. On tough days, you can revisit these pages to remind yourself of how far you've come. If you ever feel stuck or stagnant, this journal will be your proof of progress and a source of motivation to keep going. You can also incorporate these activities in your daily schedule.

The D-60 Challenge isn't just an initiative; it's a step towards a better, more mindful version of yourself. All it takes is 10 minutes a day for 60 days to gift yourself the potential for mindfulness that lasts a lifetime.

About the cover:

The cover beautifully encapsulates the essence of what this challenge aims to achieve.

In this age where information is the new gold, we keep on studying and learning new things. We strive to upgrade ourselves everyday. We bombard our minds with everything that promises success in this fast-paced world. But seldom do we pause. Seldom do we sit with ourselves and watch the chaos in our minds. Seldom do we try to disentangle the mess in our minds. Seldom do we meet us. Because amidst all the clutter, we have forgotten how to reach us.

The D-60 Challenge is a simple yet powerful collection of daily activities that will help you find your real home, you. The cover symbolizes the transformative journey of self-discovery and mindfulness that you'll undergo, offering a deeper connection with your inner selves.

<u>D-60: Journaling</u>

Today marks the 1st day of our Challenge. Sit with yourself for 5 minutes, no music, no devices, just you. After 5 minutes, write down answers for these 5 questions *without thinking*:

1. Was I happy today? Did I smile at least once?
2. Was I excited today? What were the things that excited me today?
3. Was I scared today? What were the things that scared me?
4. Was I harsh to myself today? Did I say something harsh to myself which I shouldn't have?
5. Was I goal-oriented today? Did I take at least one concrete step towards my goal/s or dream/s?

Does writing down these questions really help? Yes. Journaling is not only an effective tool of mapping one's inner thoughts, but also important from self-reflection and metacognition perspective. At the end of this D-60 Challenge, you'll not only find yourself more mindful and calm and more capable of dealing with anxiety and stress, but also have a written proof of what you did. And that really helps when you are feeling down. After this challenge ends, if you ever find yourself under stress or anxious, just go through these pages and do any of these activities. It's best if you include some of them in your daily schedule.

<u>D-59: Responsibility</u>

Today we'll list down things that overburden us. I won't call any burden trivial, because it might weigh like a huge rock for someone. But no matter how small it is, note what you feel is burdening you. After you're done writing, close your eyes and imagine all of your burdens are a rock, a boulder burdening you. Now if you're a potterhead just say Riddikulus or if you're a muggle, just imagine that rock has its own wings. It's flying away. *It is still your responsibility, but it is no longer a burden.*

What does this exercise do?

Sometimes we overburden ourselves. There might be external expectations that become a burden. Or there might be self-imposed pressure that becomes a burden.

"I am responsible for fulfilling my dream" is great. But when this responsibility becomes a burden, your dream becomes a burden, an activity that's no longer enjoyable.

"My family is my responsibility." Yes. But if you pressurize yourself with this thought, this becomes burden.

Basically, we can make this equation:
Responsibility + Pressure = Burden.

When you write these burdens down and by imagining them weightless, you're essentially removing the pressure from those burdens. You are changing the equation to: **Responsibility = Pressure - Burden**.

D-58: Affirmations

Before going to bed today, tell yourself these 9 things:

1. I do my work well every day and to the best of my ability.
2. I believe in my dreams.
3. I love myself just the way I am.
4. My happiness is my responsibility.
5. I accept my responsibilities.
6. I am ready for new beginnings.
7. There are plenty of opportunities for me in the world.
8. I am grateful to God, that energy for every day.
9. Happiness is everywhere; I want to learn to see it.

Don't dismiss affirmations saying it is some huff-puff. Affirmations work. And that is a proven psychological fact. Basically, our brain creates these neural pathways and the more repetitive thoughts have firmer pathways. This is why it takes time for us to unlearn and learn something new, add something new to our neural network.

When we say affirmations, especially on a daily basis, we are challenging those created pathways of negative thoughts including those of self-doubt.

If possible, repeat these affirmations every day. Or record yourself saying these affirmations and play that recording every day before going to bed (this is what I do).

D57 Giving your inner child small wins

Close your eyes and ask yourself this question: What do I enjoy doing? It might be staring at the sky, drinking a cup of chai by yourself, drawing, or reading a book. Every day from today, start doing that one thing for at least 5 minutes each day.

What does this do?

In our busy daily lives, we rarely do just one thing, let alone do "that one thing" which makes us happy.

When you do this one thing you love, especially every day, it'll not only recharge you and help you become more productive, but also help let that inner child live, thrive.

When you note down this one thing, try to give it at least 5 minutes of your time every day.

<u>D56 Sky Gazing</u>

Do this simple activity today. Just stare at the sky, look at the clouds, whether they are fluffy, cottony-like or whether they're creating any pattern. Look at the sky even if there are no clouds. Don't listen to any music or speak for 10 minutes while you do this. Just stare at the skies, the hues and the little changes that occur every second.

Before you go to bed, write down what thoughts you had while sky-gazing. It's okay if there was a chain of thoughts and you've forgotten a few. Whatever you remember, just write those thoughts down.

But if you had no thoughts while gazing at the sky, then there's nothing amazing than it. It sort of means that your mind was completely relaxed.

And if you had a storm of thoughts in your mind in those sky-gazing moments, that's fine too. The storm will calm down gradually. That's what we are trying to achieve in this D-60 initiative.

<u>**D55 Paying Attention**</u>

Be attentive today. When you highlight an important sentence, when you drink water, when you read and take notes, when you eat. Just pay attention to everything today. At the end of the day, write down in 10 lines about 10 things you did and how different they seemed today.

What does this achieve?

We are so used to some things that they are embedded in our muscle memory i.e. we go into machine mode with those activities.

The route I take from my home to my library has been so embedded in my mind that I don't see the lily buds have bloomed at one house on the route. I don't appreciate the bright red flowers on the *Palas* tree that are in full bloom.

When I start revising I get into the "focused mode" and forget to appreciate the beauty in the intricacy of the Indian architecture, in the words of the Indian Constitution, in the technicalities of the Economic survey.

We need to get out of this machine mode once in a while. What does appreciating the beauty in something do? It makes the churn enjoyable. You're of course walking within the confines of your schedule, your job, your deadlines, but when you start paying attention to these things you do daily and yet find a different meaning to it, you look forward to doing it again the next time to find yet another different meaning to it.

For example, when I'm paying attention while drinking water, these thoughts cross my mind: how this water has travelled through cycles, how water was from where living beings originated, and sometimes even some funny underwater story narrated by David Attenborough. It makes even drinking water an enjoyable activity.

So today when you eat, try to feel the texture of what you're eating. Try to count 32 times as you chew and then ask whether it tastes the same as it did before. **Appreciate the efforts it took for that food to reach your plate.**

<u>**D54 Breathing**</u>

What is an indication that we are alive and without what are we dead? **Breathing**.

The answer is simple, and so is the practice. But this competitive world has made us believe that simple is not right. We always go by the hard route, often ignoring that the easy and simple path is also right and will lead us to our destination as well. *"The most simple explanation is most likely true"* (Occam's Razor)

Today let us practice breathing. After reading this, start a timer of 7-10 minutes and then just close your eyes and focus on your breathing. Feel the breath filling your lungs and escaping from your nose. Don't try to control it. Let it flow into you and out of you. Be aware of its path. Be aware of how it inflates and deflates your lungs. Let these 7-10 minutes be for breathing, something that is profound and basic and yet the most effective calming pill provided to us.

Conscious Breathing is literally that one thing which helps in every situation. You might be feeling overwhelmed, conscious breathing will calm you down. You might be feeling anxious and conscious breathing will throw that anxiety out of the window (worked for me).

D53 Pet the Plants

Today's activity might seem a bit weird, but trust me it is SOOO effective and calming.

Meet the plants you have at home or if you don't, go outside and search for any random plant in your surroundings/roads/gardens/parks. Observe that plant. Look at the shade of its leaves and their shape. Look at its buds and flowers if it has any. Gently pat its leaves. Feel the texture of those leaves. Tell that plant that it's doing a good job growing. Does that feel good? If you feel good while patting a plant, why not pat your own back and tell yourself that you're doing a good job too?

How does this activity benefit YOU?

You write this down today.

It is in our nature that we seek external appreciation. And it isn't always incorrect to do so. But when you praise yourself, appreciate yourself for all that you've done until now, it'll make you sooo happy.

Write down how you felt when you patted those plants and yourself as well!

D-52 Body Scan Meditation

Today, before going to bed, lie down on yoga mat or on the floor and do a body scan meditation. Close your eyes and start focusing on your body parts in sequence. Start by paying attention to your toes, your shin area, slowly moving upwards till you focus on your forehead and then your hair.

Be slow and patient, and while you're doing this body scan, observe if there is any pain anywhere. Just observe as a third party. During scanning, be grateful to each and every body-part of yours for working so tirelessly.

Lie down in silence for a minute after this and then write it all down. Write down whether you felt anything different, anything good.

Trust me, the sleep you'll get after doing this will be out of the world!

This practice is of Yog Nidra. There's also a practice used by Psychologists called PMRT or Progressive Muscle Relaxation technique which is a more elaborate version and includes more steps. While Yog Nidra is something any one can do, PMRT is to be done under the guidance of a professional mental health care provider/psychologist.

Yog Nidra is a proven Yoga method that helps calm down one's mind and body. Yoga in general integrates one's body and mind and is like a meditation in itself. But Yog Nidra is also helpful in reducing anxiety, stress and insomnia.

You can also incorporate this in your daily schedule!
I followed Habuild Yoga's Yog Nidra guided video as a
beginner. You can find it easily on YouTube.

D-51 Rests

You're experiencing Burnout because you're not getting all types of Rests.

We've made Rests a Reward. But to continue studying/ working at your optimal capacity and avoid burnout, RESTS ARE NEEDED. There are broadly 7 types of rests:

1. Physical Rest includes: taking power naps, doing yoga and exercises, stretching for a minute or two throughout the day, taking short breaks, going for a walk.
2. Mental Rest includes: meditating, turning off your phone, digital detox/avoiding social media.
3. Emotional Rest includes: journaling, spending time with nature, talking to a friend, spending time alone, practicing self-care.
4. Sensory Rest includes: closing your eyes, deep breathing, listening to calming music, spending some time alone and in a quiet atmosphere.
5. Creative Rest includes: giving your hobby at least 5 minutes every day, taking a break to be with your thoughts.
6. Social Rest includes: having a solo-outing/date with yourself, spending some quality time alone, practicing self-care.
7. Spiritual Rest includes: Meditating, Praying, Believing (having faith), Spending time with nature, practicing Yoga.

How to practice these Rests? We have To-do lists for our tasks, include Rest in it as well. Allocate some time for it in your daily, weekly or monthly planners. There is something known as Toxic Habits and overworking yourself is one of them. Be in a healthy relationship with your studies/work. You can practice one type of rest each day. Incorporate these 7 types of Rests in your schedule today!

<u>D-50 Mindful Walking</u>

Whenever you walk today, notice each step. Be grateful that you're able to take each step towards whatever you wanted to do today.

When you journal your entry today, write down that you taking all those steps today and all the steps every day, is simply a proof that you are indeed taking one step towards your dream.

What does this activity do?

When you count even a tiny effort as that of taking one step, you are appreciating yourself right on the minutest level.

It helps you take cognizance of how tons of tiny efforts are needed for you to get through the day. And you take all those seemingly tiny efforts every day.

Aren't you amazing?!

<u>**D49 Happiness?**</u>

After watching this video, I want you to write down *at least* 5 things that make you happy. You can write as many as you can.

What does this do?

When we are sad, we are often stuck in this rut wherein we are unable to escape this vicious cycle of sadness unless some out-of-control external factor pulls us out of it, if it does.

In these sad times, we are not able to recollect what really makes us happy.

But why wait for something or someone else to pull us out of our sadness?

When you have written down what makes you happy, you can go to it when you feel sad and after a small countdown of 3..2..1.. just stop procrastinating and do whichever activity makes you happy. Give yourself that sudden jerk of happiness!

I'll list down 5 things that make me happy:

1. When I'm able to make someone laugh/when someone laughs on my joke
2. When I see new growth or a new bud or a new bloom on my plants
3. When my morning meditation session makes me content
4. When I make (my version of perfect) chai (happens rarely •ᴗ•)

5. When I pss-pss at a random cat and they
    actually let me pet them

There are many more, but I hope you get the gist. It
doesn't have to be anything grand. Just small, simple
things that make you happy and that you can practice
whenever you're feeling sad.

D48 Grounding Technique

You can do this any time today. And you can also do this whenever you're feeling overwhelmed.

Note:

5 Things you can see

4 Things you can hear

3 Things you can feel

2 Things you can smell

1 Thing you can taste

This is called Grounding Exercise.

These are the proven benefits of Grounding Exercise:

Grounding helps you reduce the feelings of overwhelm by bringing your focus back to the present. Grounding also promotes mindfulness, lowers stress levels and provides a sense of calm. These exercises enhance our awareness of our surrounding and body, which can help us feel more in control. It has been proved that Grounding can clear mental fog, thereby making it easier to concentrate. It also triggers body's relaxation response, decreasing heart rate and blood pressure. If you have anxiety, practicing grounding can help reduce the heart palpitations.

Note down this Grounding exercise and your experience after practicing!

<u>D-47 Note to Self</u>

Today, take a moment for yourself. Write these down.

Give yourself some credit today. Say these things to yourself:

1. You are worthy and lovable.
2. You are doing the best you can.
3. It's okay to ask for help when you need it.
4. Your boundaries matter, and it's okay to say no.
5. It's okay to start over and try again.
6. Your feelings are valid.
7. You are capable of amazing things.

Notes to self are like affirmations, but they're not exactly the same. When you remind yourself of these things, you're intentionally shifting your mindset toward positivity. We all need space—physically and mentally. And maintaining that internal space starts with giving yourself permission to honor those little moments of self-affirmation.

I keep these "notes to self" on sticky notes by my mirror, and honestly, it feels so good to read them daily. It's a simple but powerful reminder that *we're okay,* and *everything's going to be okay.*

Feel free to add your own affirmations or reminders to your daily list.

I'm proud of you, and I believe in you!

<u>D-46 Mindful listening to a song</u>

Listen to songs for 10 minutes today without any distractions.

What we listen to is a powerful tool. If you're listening to melancholic music, your mood will likely become a bit melancholic. If you're listening to upbeat, happy songs on repeat, it will reflect in your mood as well.

If we can wield what we listen to as a tool, we can become (self) mood manipulators.

When we are stressed, feeling anxious, or caught in a spiral of negative thoughts, listening to positive music can shift that spiral to something more uplifting and calming.

When you listen to any song today, I want you to immerse yourself in it. Feel every beat, every note, every instrument, and every word. Be a part of that song. Do this for at least 10 minutes.

After the activity, write down whether you felt a bit decluttered, if you were able to focus solely on the music, or if you noticed a shift in your mood. Also, note down the song/s that you listened to, so that you can listen to them whenever you want to manipulate your mood.

D-45 Visualization

Close your eyes, sit quietly for a minute and then visualize this:

You are living a content life, doing what you've always wanted to do. You've found your space, your home, a place where you "belong". You have the right work-life balance.

Visualize everything right upto the minutest detail including having that cup of chai. It might take 5-10 minutes, but let that sink in.

After you're done visualizing, write what you visualized. If possible, try to visualize the same thing every day.

What does this do?

Visualization as a technique has been connected with Manifestation. But it has a very deep psychological meaning. When you visualize your future, especially feeling everything through the details, it makes you less anxious about the future. It gives you a sense of calm, an assurance that everything will be okay.

When you visualize today, make sure you include your dreams, your loved ones, your ambitions and everything you want from life.

Will this change your life? I don't know.

But it will definitely change the way you deal with things, and how your mind handles every situation.

Visualization is a very powerful tool, let's use it well!

Write down your visualizations here:

D-44 Mindful Showering

Take a moment during your bath today to practice mindfulness.
Focus on the sensations - the temperature of the water, the fragrance of your soap or body gel, the softness of the lather, and the gentle touch of water on your skin. Imagine all your stress and worries being washed away with each drop of water.

Why is this important?
Mindfulness in everyday activities is essential for mental well-being. Mindful showering is a simple yet powerful way to recharge yourself.
You start your day refreshed. Practicing this in the morning can invigorate you, helping you feel more centered and ready to tackle the day.

You end your day lighter. At night, it helps release the day's accumulated stress, leaving you calmer and more relaxed.

By focusing entirely on yourself and affirming, "All my worries are being washed away", you cultivate a sense of relief and happiness. This small practice can bring noticeable peace to your routine!

<u>D-43 Savor a cup of tea/coffee</u>

Today's activity is one of my favorites.
Grab your cup of chai or coffee.
Whether you pair it with a book, some quiet reflection,
or just let it be, make this moment yours.

Feel its warmth in your hands.
Inhale its comforting aroma.
Let every sip linger—feel the texture, the taste, and the
energy it brings as it flows through you.

This isn't just a habit. It's a ritual, a small act that keeps
you whole. So today, pause and honor it. Acknowledge
its role in your life. Be grateful—not just for the cup in
your hand but for the people who made it possible.

And after you savor it, take a moment to reflect. Write
down how it made you feel, what it stirred within you.
Let's celebrate the beauty in the simplest moments!

D-42 Laugh.

Today's activity is simple and fun: laugh.

Watch a stand-up, a comedy clip, or try one of my
personal favorites—watch funny animal videos or
laugh for no reason at all. Yes, it might feel silly, and
no, it doesn't make you crazy.

Why is this important?
Laughter is freedom. Whether it's sparked by a joke or
comes out of nowhere, it lets you release control and
just be. It's also nature's way of giving us a boost—
releasing dopamine and serotonin to lighten your mood
and energize your spirit.

Think about it: when kids laugh for no reason, no one
calls them crazy. So why should you care if someone
thinks you're a little "childish"? Maybe that's exactly
what we all need—a break from overthinking, from
worrying about judgments, from holding ourselves
back.

So today, let go of those inhibitions. Forget about "what
will they think" and just laugh. Laugh loudly, laugh
freely, laugh unapologetically.

And when you're done, take a moment to reflect: Did
you feel lighter? Freer? Or maybe nothing at all?
Whatever you felt, write it down.

D-41 Mindful Doodling

Today's activity is Mindful Doodling. Take any blank sheet of paper and a pen of your choice, and start making patterns.

Art therapy is a proven practice in psychology. While we won't delve into it right now, doodling, in my experience, is an activity that can help you become mindful. When you draw certain patterns and create art out of them, especially intricate ones, your mind becomes fully engaged in the process. You can try Mandala art or simple doodling. It doesn't have to be grand and you don't have to use the best art paper and pens. You don't even have to show your art to anyone - it's just for you. If you feel mindful and a bit thoughtless while doing this activity today, then whenever your mind feels chaotic and you need a mental break, simply take a pen and paper and start drawing patterns. There's no one to judge your art. In fact, art is beyond judgement - it's a form of expression.

So, express yourself today and whenever you feel mentally overworked.

<u>**D-40 Self-Reflection**</u>

You have been doing this challenge for almost 20 days now. Congratulations for being consistent and sticking to this. I'm proud of you!

Today, let us reflect on how far we've come in these 20 days. You can choose to close your eyes and make mental notes, or you can jot this down. Note the changes you have seen in yourself in these 20 days. There will be at least one. Are you feeling calm? Are you feeling less anxious? Are you feeling more (goal-) oriented? Write it all down. Let today be the day when you talk to yourself, have a dialogue with yourself.

<u>D-39 Writing your worries away</u>

What are you worried about? What scares you? Are you afraid of something?

I want you to write at least 5 things that you're worried/scared/afraid about. You can list down all of them if you want to. Don't think about whether they are trivial or not. Don't think about whether they are too grand for you to worry about. They are your fears, acknowledge them. Try to list all of them down, trust me it'll help you.

I'll list down mine for reference (and for transparency):

1. I have a deep fear of failure -(I work so hard and I used to face burnouts because I don't want to fail)
2. I'm worried that the succulent pup I planted last week might not survive
3. I'm scared of uncertainty. Will my Plan B work? Will I be able to make it my career?
4. I'm worried that my favorite pen has gone out of stock and I won't be able to get it anymore (yes, it scares me)
5. I'm afraid that afterlife might not be close to the 'heaven' and 'hell' we have been told about

I'm just listing 5 out of my many fears. But you get the idea, right?

List down all of your fears and worries, no one but you gets to see them. But writing them down is an important part of the process. And yes, it will be challenging to do, but if you get out of your comfort zone and learn to acknowledge things about yourself that make you uncomfortable, that's where your growth begins.

The fun part comes out tomorrow!!

D-38 Mind Cleaning

Based on yesterday's writing off your worries, we'll do another activity today. Sit with yourself and the worries you had written about yesterday. Now imagine that with every breath you exhale, your worries are going away and with every breath you inhale, you are gaining strength to tackle the challenges that come your way. Set a timer and do this for at least 7 minutes. You can do this for whatever time you want to. What does this do?

We may not realize but we are worried about many small things. Yes, the big things are scary as well, but it is these small worries that go unnoticed which clutter our mind and make us even more anxious.

Will this activity stop you from getting worried? NO. It's in our nature to get worried. Some people get more worried than others. And that's fine.

But when we write down things that are worrying us, weighing us down, we are acknowledging the monster in the room. That's the most important task. When you do this activity, you let go of these worries. And yes, new worries will accumulate in your mind again, just like our room gets dirty some days after we have cleaned it. Hence, this activity is something we have to do periodically, just like cleaning our rooms.

After doing this activity, write down how you felt!

D-37 Physical Decluttering

Take some time today to clean your room, especially your study space. As you do this, avoid listening to music or any distractions—immerse yourself fully in the act of cleaning.

Why does this matter?

When you clean your space mindfully, think of it as more than just tidying up. Picture the dust you're wiping away as the clutter in your mind—each sweep or wipe clears away negativity and unnecessary thoughts. As you discard things you no longer need, imagine you're letting go of mental baggage too.

Our elders often remind us of the importance of a clean room, and for good reason: a clean, organized environment naturally enhances focus and clarity. Yesterday, we worked on decluttering our minds; today, let's extend that to our physical surroundings.

By cleaning your space, you're signaling to your mind that you're ready for change. This simple act creates a productive environment, reduces procrastination, and helps combat laziness.

Trust me, once you've finished, you'll not only see the difference—you'll *feel* it.

<u>**D-36 Box Breathing**</u>

Today, I want you to try this simple yet powerful technique:

- Inhale for a count of 4.
- Hold your breath for a count of 4.
- Exhale for a count of 4.
- Hold your breath again for a count of 4.
- Repeat this cycle for at least 5 minutes.

This practice is called Box Breathing, and it's a technique that not only helps in moments of anxiety or stress but also, when done consistently, can significantly improve your mindfulness and emotional regulation.

Just like the breathing exercise we practiced earlier, this one is essential for cultivating calm and focus. Whenever you feel yourself spiraling—whether it's overthinking, overreacting, or feeling anxious or angry—turn to this simple rhythm of breath. It's a grounding tool to pause and regain clarity.

Once you're done, take a moment to reflect. Write down how you felt during and after the exercise. Did your thoughts slow down? Did you notice a sense of calm creeping in?

Give it a try—you might be surprised at how much it helps.

<u>D-35 Humming</u>

Today's activity is simple: humming.

Choose any song you like—hum it on your own or put on your earphones and hum along. Don't worry about what anyone else might think; this is your moment. Spend at least 5 minutes humming, and feel free to repeat it as often as you want throughout the day.

Why is this important?

Humming is something we often do unconsciously—like when a tune gets stuck in our heads for weeks. Chances are, you've caught yourself humming it without even realizing. This natural act isn't just random; it's a form of relaxation (yes, it has been psychologically proven as well). That's why we hum lullabies to babies—to soothe and calm them.

Today, give yourself the same gift. Let the act of humming ease your mind and lighten your mood. Before going to bed, take a moment to reflect: Did humming make you feel even a little happier? It doesn't have to be life-changing, and your thoughts may not disappear entirely, but if it brought a moment of joy or calmness, consider making this a daily habit.

D-34 Just Dance!

Today, your challenge is simple: put on your favorite song and dance however you like. Forget about being a "good dancer" or worrying about what others might think—this is just for you. Let go of any hesitation. If it helps, dance alone in your room where no one's watching. Let yourself feel free and carefree, even if it's just for one song.

Why is this important?

Like the other D-60 activities, this is about breaking free from the thoughts that hold you back. Dancing freely, without judgment or fear, helps you:

- Release self-imposed limitations and embrace your unique self.
- Boost your mood through the simple joy of moving to music.
- Build self-confidence by stepping outside your comfort zone.

When you do the things you normally shy away from, you break down those invisible walls you've built around yourself. It's a small act, but it can lead to big changes in how you feel and see the world.

After you're done, pause and reflect:

- Did you feel lighter, happier, or freer?
- What did it feel like to let go, even for a moment?

Write down your thoughts and celebrate the small victories—they're worth it!

D-33 See a Sunset

Take a moment to watch the Sunset today.

Notice how the colors shift and blend across the sky, creating a masterpiece that changes with every passing second. You can pair this experience with a song or simply enjoy it in silence, letting it be just you and your thoughts.

Why does this matter?

Nature has an incredible power to heal us. The more we connect with it, the more we nurture not just our physical health but our mental well-being too. Watching a sunset, with its ever-changing hues, feels like a reset button for the soul. It melts away the fatigue of the day and wraps you in a moment of pure magic.

In that fleeting moment, you're reminded of the vastness of life—the grand scheme of things. Something so breathtaking happens every single day, yet we often overlook it in the rush of our lives. "I don't have time" might feel like a valid excuse, but the truth is, we always find time for what truly matters. So today, make time for this sunset.

As you watch, write down your thoughts. Describe the colors, the patterns, the feeling of being present. Capture the moment on paper as if you're painting it with words. And later, even if life gets busy, revisit your notes. Let that simple observation remind you of the peace and magic that nature offers, waiting for you every single day.

D-32 Be kind to someone today (and every day if possible •ᴗ•)

Practice Kindness Today

Kindness is a gift we can all give. Commit to at least one act of kindness—whether it's helping an elderly person cross the street, leaving a thoughtful note for someone, or offering a genuine compliment.

Why does this matter?

In a world filled with trolling and negativity, especially on social media, genuine kindness is rare yet powerful. Toxic environments—both online and offline—can take a toll on our well-being. So, ask yourself: When was the last time I was truly kind to someone?

Take a moment to reflect:

1. Do I have any toxic traits I criticize in others?
2. Am I the kind of person I wish others would be to me?

We all crave kindness, support, and encouragement, but are we offering the same to others?

Start small, but make it a habit. Practice kindness not just today but every chance you get.

What you give to the world often finds its way back to you.

D-31 Smile at Strangers

This might look embarrassing, but smile at people you know as well as random strangers today. Try to smile at people you've had brief eye contact with. They might take you for a fool, but you aren't going to meet them again anyway. You never know what someone is going through. That one smile from you might just make their day!

When we do activities like these that make us cross our comfort zones, we might feel uncomfortable at first, and that's natural. But once you start crossing these so-called mental boundaries within which you've confined yourself, you'll realize that you can achieve anything and everything—you just have to cross the barrier with the sign "You won't be able to do this."

There's another gain from doing activities like these: we feel happy and content. In our everyday lives, where work or studies, goals, and aspirations have consumed us, where we've forgotten to truly be alive, these activities help us reconnect to what makes us, us.

Kindness has a habit of coming back to its source. Be the source.

D-30 Notes of Gratitude

Write a heartfelt note to someone close – someone you don't thank enough. It could be your parents, your best friends or anyone who's been there for you. If you're comfortable, call them to express your gratitude or if that feels a bit awkward, simply write a message or note and send it to them.

In the winding journey of life, there are people who stand by us during our lowest moments and help us rise to our highest. Sometimes we thank them, and sometimes we silently carry that gratitude in our hearts.

But today, let's take a moment to turn those unspoken feelings into words. Let these people know how much they truly mean to us.

When you make this a habit – expressing gratitude not just once but at least once a year – it grounds you. It reminds you that you're not alone, that your journey has been supported by the love and care of others. Gratitude also helps you reflect on your growth, while letting those around you feel valued and appreciated.

This simple act can spark mindfulness – not just for you, but for the people around you.
Let them know they matter.

<u>D-29 Book reading</u>.

Take 10 minutes today—just 10—and pick up any book that calls to you. Fiction, non-fiction, poetry, or any genre you like. Set a timer, dive into its pages, and let yourself get lost in its world for those precious moments.

Why does this matter?

Writers dedicate years to crafting stories, ideas, and knowledge that add meaning to our lives. I'm not here to turn you into an avid reader if you're not one, but think about this: If you read just one book a year, by the end of your life, you'll have countless new worlds, lessons, and perspectives under your belt. If you read one a month, that's 12 books a year—12 chances to grow, escape, or discover.

From a mindfulness perspective, reading does more than entertain; it's an act of self-care. It gives your mind a break from the grind, refuels your creativity, and helps you avoid burnout. You're not just flipping pages; you're investing in yourself.

D-28 Notice your Surroundings

Notice your surroundings today. Observe little things. How cold/warm did the weather feel? How many plants grew new leaves? Are the sunsets getting prettier?

What does this do?

This activity makes you attentive. We look at everything around us, but do we really notice everything around us?

This activity teaches us to pay attention. When you pay attention and notice something different in the same surroundings it indicates changes in something seemingly permanent.

Isn't that a life lesson in itself? That change is inevitable? That if your life feels like same day repeating itself on loop, something new will happen? Something new might've started happening already - you just haven't been paying attention?

Write down what you noticed in your surroundings and subsequently *yourself*.

<u>**D-27 Mindful Self Check-ins**</u>

Ask yourself multiple times throughout the day *"How am I doing right now?"*

Note down these observations. These are 'Mindful Self Check-ins'.

In a world overflowing with information, aspirations, and expectations, we often lose touch with ourselves. We're constantly looking outward, chasing the next goal or meeting the next demand. But when was the last time you truly checked in with you?

Take today as an opportunity to shift your focus inward. Ask yourself this question multiple times. Write down your answers.

Why? Because unless we recognize the storms or calm within us, we can't navigate life effectively.

Mindful Self Check-ins help you:

1. Tune into your thoughts and emotions.
2. Gauge your deeper sense of well-being.
3. Build awareness—the crucial first step to growth and healing.

When you note down how you're feeling throughout the day, you'll uncover patterns and truths that often go unnoticed. Whether you're thriving or struggling, this practice empowers you to better understand and care for yourself.

Awareness is always the first step.

D-26 Shavasana

Today, let's practice Shavasana—a favorite for many, yet often misunderstood. While it may appear simple, Shavasana is not just lying down or taking a nap. Like every other Yogasana, Shavasana also integrates the body and mind into one plane. The word Shavasana comes from *Shava* (meaning "dead body") and *Asana* (meaning "pose"). The practice involves lying down as still and detached as a corpse—not in a morbid sense, but as a metaphor for surrendering all distractions and attachments.

How to Practice Shavasana:

- Perform some light yoga or stretching beforehand to relax your muscles and maximize the benefits.
- Use a yoga mat to ensure comfort and alignment.
- Start with 10 minutes. This ensures you don't fall asleep while keeping the practice intentional.
- Lie flat on your back with your arms relaxed by your sides, palms facing the ceiling.
- Let your legs naturally fall open and release all tension in your body.
- Silently tell yourself: "For these 10 minutes, I am nothing." Truly believe it.
- Observe your thoughts without attachment—let them drift like clouds passing in the sky or breaths leaving your body.

- When the timer ends, roll onto your right side, allowing your body to transition gently.
- Sit up slowly, open your eyes, and take a moment to feel gratitude for the practice.

Shavasana can be practiced daily, especially after an intense workout or yoga session, or before bed for improved relaxation.

Benefits of Shavasana:

- Physical Relaxation: Relieves fatigue, reduces muscle tension, and calms the nervous system.
- Mental Clarity: Encourages non-judgmental observation of thoughts, promoting self-awareness.
- Stress Reduction: Lowers cortisol levels, alleviates anxiety, and restores emotional balance.
- Improved Sleep: Prepares the body and mind for restful sleep, combating insomnia and restlessness.
- Focus and Mindfulness: Anchors you in the present moment, improving concentration and awareness.

But above all, Shavasana creates a sacred space for introspection, allowing you to witness your thoughts as a neutral observer. It's a practice of surrender, clarity, and inner peace.

Take these 10 minutes today and experience the profound stillness Shavasana offers. You are not just lying down—you are letting go.

<u>D-25 Self hugging</u>

Take a moment to wrap yourself in a tight hug today.
As you do, gently remind yourself of these truths:

- I am capable of achieving my dreams.
- I am enough, just as I am.
- I am proud of myself.
- I trust myself completely.
- I am deeply loved.
- I love myself wholeheartedly.

Why does this matter?

We all seek validation—it's natural. Sometimes, we wish for someone to tell us we're enough, that we're loved, and that we're capable of incredible things. But why wait for someone else? Give yourself that validation. Say these affirmations out loud. Acknowledge how far you've come, the challenges you've faced, and the growth you've achieved. It's easy to be consumed by thoughts of "not enough"—not doing enough, not achieving enough. But these thoughts are shaped by societal pressures that tie our worth to accomplishments.

The truth is, you are enough without needing to prove anything. You are loved, even without meeting traditional definitions of success.

So today, hold yourself close and speak to yourself with the kindness and reassurance you'd offer a child. Whisper to yourself: *It's okay. Everything is going to be okay.*

<u>D-24 Shaking exercise</u>

Try this: Shake it out!

Bring your hands to the front.
Wiggle your fingers and toes.
Start shaking your hands, then add soft jumps to shake
out your legs.
Let go of any patterns – move however your body
wants to. Shake freely and spontaneously, as if your
whole being is loosening up.
Shaking is a simple yet powerful exercise to calm your
nervous system.
The lack of structure allows your mind to experience a
sense of freedom, breaking away from rigidity. It
reconnects you with your inner child, that playful,
uninhibited part of you that craves expression.
No long explanations today.
Just try it. Let your body move without overthinking,
and then write down how you felt during and after.
Let yourself be free.

D-23 Write with your Non-Dominant Hand

Today's activity is all about stepping out of your comfort zone. If you're right-handed, try writing with your left hand, and if you're left-handed, switch to your right.

This exercise embodies the core idea of the D60 Challenge: breaking set patterns. Through this journey, we aim to challenge the routines and habits that shape our everyday lives, encouraging us to embrace discomfort and explore untapped potential.

Why does this matter? Because when we try something unfamiliar, we not only expand our abilities but also open our minds to new possibilities. These small challenges build the confidence to say, *"If I set my mind to it, I can do it."*

So today, as you write with your non-dominant hand, you're challenging a habit that's been ingrained since childhood. Pick a piece of literature, a poem, or a quote close to your heart, and write it down with your non-dominant hand.

Let the experience remind you: *growth begins where comfort ends.*

<u>**D-22 Think before you speak**</u>

Today's activity is a challenging one: pause and think before you speak—every single time.

Why are we doing this?
Life often throws us into situations where it's easy to lose our calm and react impulsively. While reacting might feel natural in the moment, it can lead to regret later. How many times have you found yourself wondering if you overreacted or wishing you had chosen your words more carefully?

Here's the challenge:
Before you speak, pause. Reflect on what you were about to say. Ask yourself, "Is this necessary? Is it kind? Is it constructive?"
Only speak once you've calmed down and are sure of your response.
By practicing mindful communication, you can avoid unnecessary conflicts, build better relationships, and align your words with your intentions.

Reflection task:
At the end of the day, take a few moments to write down your experiences.
Did you notice a difference in your interactions?
Were there moments where pausing changed the outcome?
How did it make you feel?
If you found this practice helpful, consider making it a part of your everyday life. Remember, *mindful communication is a skill that can transform not just your words, but your relationships and your peace of mind.*

D-21 Time mapping

Do you ever wonder why despite having a perfect plan, you struggle to execute it?

Here's what you need to do:

1. Write down every activity you do today, no matter how small—brushing your teeth, studying, phone calls, etc.
2. Record how much time each activity takes. Be as detailed as possible.

This exercise, called time mapping, reveals how you actually spend your time. Often, we unknowingly devote too much time to tasks that don't require it, leaving us with unfinished goals and a lingering sense of regret. For example, it took me 15 minutes to prepare and drink my Chai, but I managed to read the newspaper during that time.

What you'll discover:

1. Which activities consume more time than necessary.
2. Where you're losing time to distractions like social media or prolonged breaks.
3. Opportunities to multitask effectively or streamline certain routines.

Time mapping is a foundational step in effective planning, but it's often overlooked. By doing this exercise today, you'll gain clarity on where your time goes and identify areas to cut down gradually.

D-20 Self-Reflection

You've completed 40 days of this incredible journey—only 20 more to go! Congratulations! I'm so proud of how far you've come.

Today is a milestone, and just like we did on D-40, let's take some time to pause, reflect, and celebrate your progress.

Here's what to do:

1. Revisit what you wrote during D-40's Self-Reflection activity.

2. Reflect on these questions:
   - How much have you changed since then?
   - In what ways have you grown over the past 40 days?
   - What challenges have you overcome, and what lessons have you learned?

Why this matters:

Growth is always gradual. It's easy to overlook how far you've come when you're focused on the end goal. But every small step, every effort you've made, has brought you closer to becoming your best self.

Celebrate the progress you've made, no matter how big or small. Let this reflection remind you of your strength and resilience, and use it as fuel to power through the next 20 days.

You're closer than you think—keep going!

D19 Label your emotions

You can do this throughout the day or at the end of the day. Label your emotions today. Take some time out to acknowledge what you're feeling. Recognize and label your emotions. *"I am feeling frustrated"*, *"I am feeling motivated"*, etc. Identify and write down all these emotions.

Why is it important?

Sometimes there's a disconnection between our rational mind and our emotional mind. This disconnection can not only cause mental breakdowns if not recognized, but also impair our ability to take good decisions. To bridge this gap between the brain and the mind/heart, between thought and feeling, we need to label emotions. Instead of pushing away difficult emotions or overly analyzing them, try accepting them without judgement. Acknowledge your feelings as valid, even if they don't seem to make sense. This helps to create a harmony between your rational and emotional brain.

Feelings, when given a thought, become emotions and emotions when acknowledged makes one's heart, one's inner child feel validated. So when you label your emotions, you heal that inner child, make it happy.

Choose to be happy. Make this effort to be happy.

D-18 What I don't like about myself

There's only one thing stopping you from growing:
How you perceive yourself.
Today, challenge yourself to step into discomfort. Take a moment to write down the things you don't like about yourself. Yes, it will feel uneasy—but that's the point. I'll repeat: *Growth begins where comfort ends.*

Why is this important?
We often fall into two extremes:

1. Overcritical self-bullying – constantly pressuring and tearing ourselves down.
2. Overindulgent sugarcoating – ignoring flaws under the guise of self-love.

Both tendencies are toxic. True self-love lies in balance: accepting who you are while being honest about what needs to change.

When reflecting today, if nothing comes to mind, think about how you treat others. Would you want to be treated the same way? Step into their shoes and identify any behaviors or traits you wouldn't appreciate.

This exercise is designed to push you out of your comfort zone. Discomfort is temporary, but the growth it leads to is transformative.

Write with complete honesty.

<u>**D-17 Replacement**</u>

Yesterday, we took a moment to write down the things we don't like about ourselves.

Today, let's take it a step further—let's transform those negatives into positives! Instead of focusing on what we dislike, we'll reframe them as strengths or opportunities for growth.

For example:
"I don't like that I'm an overthinker" becomes **"I use overthinking to explore different perspectives and develop a holistic view."**
"I don't look nice" becomes **"I look nice to myself, and that's all that matters. I don't need to fit someone else's idea of beauty."**
"I don't like that I'm dominating" becomes **"I have the ability to take charge and make decisions confidently."**

The key is not to eliminate these traits but to *shift your perspective*. Even so-called "toxic traits" can be turned around. For instance:
"I'm too talkative and not a good listener" can be reframed as "I enjoy initiating conversations, and I'll work on improving my listening skills."

Often, the things we dislike about ourselves aren't inherently bad—they're just misunderstood or mismanaged. Ask yourself why you dislike those traits. Is it because you're overthinking or comparing yourself to others?

By changing the *why*, you change the *how*—how you see yourself and how you feel about those traits. Embrace the process of turning self-doubt into self-love!

D-16 My Rainbow

Let's draw a rainbow today! It doesn't need to be perfect—just include the seven colors of a rainbow. In each color, write down one thing that's precious to you.

Once you're done, place your rainbow somewhere you can see it—on your study desk or in the notebook you're using. Underneath it, take a moment to write why these people or things are so precious to you.

Why is this important?
Just like looking at a rainbow fills us with hope, these people and things add those colors and that hope to your life. When you write down your rainbow, you create a reminder of who and what to turn to when grey clouds fill your sky.

Here's my rainbow:
R: God, who created me and everything that makes me who I am—my dreams, hobbies, and more.
O: My parents.
Y: My best friends.
G: My plants.
B: Chai and panipuri.
I: Art, books, and songs.
V: BTS.

Now it's your turn!

Draw your rainbow here:

D-15 What Excites Me?

Take a moment to jot down at least 10 things that bring you joy or excitement. It could be anything—an impromptu pani puri treat, a cozy evening with your favorite book, or an adventurous trek. Big or small, ordinary or extraordinary, write them all down.

Why does this matter?

We live in an age of constant dopamine hits—be it through social media, binge-watching, or endless notifications. While these give us instant gratification, they often dull our excitement for the simple, meaningful joys of life.

By writing down what excites you, you're creating a personalized list of happiness triggers. The next time you feel low or tempted to scroll for a quick dopamine fix, pick something from your list instead. Let these moments of joy be your long-lasting, mindful remedy for a happier, more fulfilling life.

<u>D-14 What do I like about myself?</u>

Are you caught in the trap of low self-confidence? Today's activity is your way out. Take a moment to write down at least 7 things you genuinely like about yourself.

Why this matters:
In a previous activity, we focused on identifying what we don't like about ourselves. But today, let's flip the script. Think about what you appreciate about yourself—no matter how big or small.

It could be something about your appearance, your personality, or even your quirks. For instance, I love how I can switch from cracking puns to reflecting deeply on God and faith in the blink of an eye.

What does this achieve?
When you acknowledge the things you like about yourself, you're building a foundation of self-acceptance and confidence. These qualities make you unique and capable.

If you can list at least 7 things you admire about yourself, isn't that proof enough that you're ready to take on life's challenges? *Confidence begins with liking yourself for who you are.* This positive mindset becomes the material for the ladder that leads to your success.

So, start writing and remember:
You are your greatest asset.

D-13 Reading a poem, Appreciating a Poet

Take a moment today to read a poem and celebrate the art of poetry.

Poetry, in its essence, is art woven with words—a canvas where thoughts are painted, sometimes with rhymes and rhythms, sometimes without. When you immerse yourself in a poem, pause to feel the weight of its words. What story are they telling? What emotions are they carrying? Allow yourself to resonate with the poet's voice, to absorb the message that unfolds between the lines.

Poetry has the power to shift perspectives, to inspire, and sometimes, to transform lives. Here's a poem that became a turning point in my own journey:

THE PERSON I'M LOOKING FOR....

If you do not get lowered in your eyes
While you raise yourself in those of others
If you do not give in to gossips and lies
Rather heed them not, saying, 'who bothers?'
You may be the person I'm looking for.

If you crave not for praise when you win
And look not for sympathy while you lose
If cheers let not your head toss or spin
And after a setback you offer no excuse
You may be the person I'm looking for.

If you accept counsel without getting sore
And re-assess yourself in the light there-of
If you pledge not be obstinate anymore

And meet others without any frown or scoff
You may be the person I'm looking for.

If you have the will to live and courage to die
You are a beacon-light for people far & wide
If you ignore the jeers and, thus expose the lie 'That
virtue and success do not go side by side'
You are the person I'm looking for.

-Hazara Singh.

Write down some lines from the poem/s you read
today:

<u>**D-12 Mindful doodling AGAIN.**</u>

Today's activity is Mindful Doodling. Take any blank sheet of paper and a pen of your choice, and start making patterns.

We've done this activity before, and you can revisit what you created last time.
I've included this activity again because doodling is a powerful tool for cultivating mindfulness. When you doodle—whether it's patterns, shapes, or free-flowing designs—your mind becomes fully engaged in the process. This focused attention helps quiet the racing thoughts in your mind and, at times, even gives you a moment of stillness.

Today, before you begin doodling, try a quick box breathing session. This simple breathing exercise will help center your focus and allow you to be more present with your art. Notice how the combination of mindful breathing and doodling enhances your sense of calm and clarity.

D-11 Cooking

You might not consider yourself a great cook, but today, I want you to prepare something for yourself. It could be something as simple as Maggi, ramen, or even a full meal—whatever feels manageable.

The real activity here is not just cooking but being present in the process. When you're chopping vegetables, focus on the rhythm of the knife. As you add spices or masalas, pause to inhale their rich aroma. Notice how the water boils, how the noodles soften, and how the ingredients transform with heat.

Why is this important?

Food has been a constant companion throughout our evolution. It's primal, a source of comfort that predates even our ability to stand upright. This connection is why we often turn to food during times of stress—it soothes us on a deep, instinctive level.

Today, immerse yourself in this act of cooking. Engage all your senses and observe how the simple act of preparing food brings calm to your body and mind. Let it ground you, reconnect you, and remind you of the comfort food has always provided.

D-10 Pamper Yourself

Today, take some time to pamper yourself. It doesn't have to revolve around food or drinks—choose something that brings you joy. Maybe it's visiting a stationery shop and picking out a pen you love. Perhaps it's lying in bed, listening to your favorite music, or immersing yourself in a Studio Ghibli or Pixar movie. Whatever it is, make it something *just for you.*

Why does this matter?
We often go out of our way to do things for others, but when was the last time you did something special for yourself? Caring for others is wonderful, but to keep that care-giving "power bank" charged, you need to care for yourself too.

When you pamper yourself, you're sending a powerful signal to your subconscious: I matter. I am important. I am worth taking care of. Over time, this simple act of self-care can do more than recharge you—it can boost your mindfulness, nurture your well-being, and elevate your self-confidence.

Today, write down how you chose to pamper yourself and reflect on how it made you feel. Small steps like these can lead to a deeper appreciation for yourself and the care you truly deserve.

<u>D-9 Random calls</u>

Today, pick up your phone and make a few calls—
random, meaningful, or unexpected. Call your friends
or family members and chat about anything that comes
to mind. Share stories, ask about their lives, and maybe
even brag a little about this challenge you're doing.
You could even reach out to a long-lost friend and
simply ask, *"How have you been?"*
Go beyond yourself today and connect.

Why does this matter?
Mindfulness is something we cultivate within, but just
like a seed in the soil needs sunlight and water to grow,
the mindfulness we're nurturing also needs its
nourishment—hope, connection, and affection.
And here's the beautiful part: as much as we need that
nourishment, we can also be that nourishment for
others. Be someone's sunlight today, their drop of
water, their moment of kindness.
We often hear that we must love ourselves first before
loving others, but love doesn't have to follow a
sequence or hierarchy. You can love others and love
yourself at the same time—fully, equally, and without
limitation. That's how the seed of mindfulness truly
thrives.

So, let today's calls, no matter how random they seem,
carry a clear intention: *to connect, to care, and to love.*

D-8 2 Js: Jump and Joke.

Today's activities are all about fun: Jump and Joke.

When you jump, you're not just getting your heart rate up or releasing a burst of adrenaline—you're reconnecting with pure, childlike joy. That feeling of lightness, as if you've been transported back to your carefree childhood, is a beautiful way to reconnect with your inner child.

And then, crack some jokes. Silly, lame, or downright ridiculous—let them flow! Laugh at your own jokes, share them with friends, and don't hold back. Don't hesitate to share your creativi-tea.

Let today be filled with laughter, playfulness, and light-hearted moments. Jump, joke, and let your inner child take center stage—because they deserve this day of joy.

<u>**D-7 Pray**</u>

Today, take a moment to pray or reflect—whichever resonates with you. If you believe in a higher power, have a conversation with them. If you're an atheist, sit quietly with yourself and connect inward. But this time, don't ask for anything.

We often approach prayer with requests: "Please give me this," or "Help me with that." But have we ever paused to ask the divine how they are? Have we ever wondered if they feel burdened by the weight of countless lives and endless demands? Do they feel disappointed watching us harm nature? Do they, like us, experience sadness or loneliness?

Today, be a friend to God. Yes, the divine exists on a level far beyond our understanding, but imagine for a moment that you could ease their loneliness, even a little. Approach this connection not as a seeker, but as someone offering kindness, curiosity, and companionship.

Let this activity remind you that you are not alone. You are deeply connected—to something higher, vaster, and more profound than you can comprehend. Let this be a moment of stillness, a moment of connection, and a moment of peace between yourself and the infinite.

D-6 Boundaries

Today, take the time to draw your boundaries—clearly and unapologetically. Write them down. These are your lines, your safe space, and when this challenge ends, I want you to remind yourself daily: "These are my boundaries, and I will not let anyone cross them."

Boundaries look different for everyone. For example, I dislike it when relatives constantly question me about my career, but someone else might not mind. It's subjective, and that's okay. What matters is identifying where you don't want others to interfere. Write it down—what behaviours, questions, or situations make you uncomfortable or feel violated?

Remember, people who do good work are often rewarded with more work. While it may seem flattering, overworking yourself harms your mental health and sets a dangerous precedent where people start taking you for granted. Protect yourself by learning to say NO.

<u>D-5 Highlight yourself</u>

Today, it's time to highlight yourself. Why?
Because *YOU ARE IMPORTANT*.

Jokes aside, today's activity is about self-reflection and
recognizing your own worth. Take a moment to do a
self-analysis:

Write down adjectives that describe you—words that
reflect who you truly are. For example: I am
compassionate, responsible, considerate, empathetic,
dependable, truthful, sincere, and so on.

These words are more than just descriptors; they are
your highlights—the qualities that make you, you. They
may not always be visible to others, but they are your
intangible assets, a reflection of your inner strength and
value.

Whenever you find yourself questioning your self-
worth, return to this entry. Read these words. Let them
remind you of your essence, your goodness, and your
importance. You are more than enough, and these
highlights prove it.

D-4 My dream, My responsibility

Today's activity is about taking full responsibility for your dreams.

Start by writing down all your dreams—big or small, short-term or long-term, practical or idealistic. Whether it's clearing an exam, making a difference in the world, wiping tears from someone's eyes, or helping others fulfill their dreams—put them all on paper.

Once you've created your dream list, write this in bold, capital letters:
MY DREAMS ARE MY RESPONSIBILITY.

Let this be your reminder: no one else can fulfil your dreams for you. No one else can climb the ladder, take the next step, push you beyond your comfort zone, or challenge you to grow. Only you can do that. Your dreams are yours to fight for, and you are capable of achieving them.

The galaxies in your eyes shine because of these dreams—don't let that sparkle fade. Stand up for yourself and for what you believe in. Yes, the journey may be hard. Yes, you may have stumbled or faced failure. But remember: FAIL simply means First Attempt In Learning. Embrace the lesson, rise stronger, and fight harder for your dreams.

From today onward, promise yourself this: I will accomplish my dreams. Be the person your future self will look back on with gratitude and pride.
Your dreams are worth it—and so are you.

D-3 Positivi-tea

Make yourself a cup of chai or coffee. With each sip
that you take, repeat these:

1. I am enough
2. I can do everything I want to do
3. I can achieve everything I dream of
4. I have the strength to tackle the challenges on
   my way
5. I can turn obstacles into opportunities
6. I believe in myself
7. I love myself

Repeat these till you finish your chai or coffee.

Affirmations can significantly boost self-confidence, a
fact many of us are already aware of. However, making
them a consistent part of our daily routine can be
challenging. The key to integrating affirmations into
your life is to pair them with something you already do
regularly. For instance, if having a cup of chai or coffee
is a ritual in your day, use that moment to say your
affirmations. Let your beverage not only recharge your
body and brain but also infuse your mind with
positivity. Turn that sip of tea or coffee into a moment
of self-empowerment!

D-2 Self-love and Self-belief

Today's activity is designed to help you embrace and embody the true essence of self-love and self-belief. Reflect on the below lines, absorb their essence and write down your thoughts after soaking it all in.

Self-love and self-belief are the hidden jewels of our lives, enriching us in proportion to how we nurture and embrace them. While the concept of self-love is often discussed, we rarely pause to truly reflect on what it means to love ourselves.

Loving oneself begins with recognizing how fortunate we are to even have the capacity for self-love. As conscious beings, we have the power to rewrite our stars through our subconscious thoughts, the thoughts we knowingly or unknowingly cultivate.

Understanding that there are no limits to our potential and daring to venture into the unknown with that belief is what it means to truly love ourselves. True self-love is not about ignoring our flaws or shortcomings, but acknowledging them with compassion and striving to grow. It's about improving, not masking, who we are. In doing so, we cultivate self-belief.

If self-love is the force that heals us, self-belief is the strength that propels us forward, allowing us to rise, take action, and pursue our goals. Together, an amalgamation of these two elements weave the magic of mindfulness into our lives, transforming our journey with every step.

D-1 Journaling

Today marks the last day of our Challenge. I want you to do today's activity only after you've done all the previous activities.

We'll be repeating something we have done on the very first day of this challenge. Sit with yourself for 5 minutes, no music, no devices, just you.

Without thinking, write down the answers for these 5 questions.

1. Was I happy today? Did I smile at least once?
2. Was I excited today? What were the things that excited me today?
3. Was I scared/afraid today? What were the things that scared me?
4. Was I harsh to myself today? Did I say something harsh to myself which I shouldn't have? What did I say?
5. Was I goal-oriented today? Did I take at least one concrete step towards my goal/s or dreams?

After writing the answers to these questions, I want you to go back to the first entry: the D-60 entry, where we had answered these same questions. Are your answers different?

If yes, then reflect on them. Why did they become different? Which activities from these D-60 Challenge have you incorporated in your daily schedule? Did following these activities consistently help change these answers?

If not, then reflect on them. Have you incorporated at least one activity from these activities in your schedule? If you haven't yet, I want you to do so.

If your answer to the 1st question was the same as before, I want you to include any of these activities in your daily schedule:

1. Watch a stand-up comedy video or a funny video for at least 5 minutes everyday
2. If you like nature, watch any episode of Our Earth or related documentaries for at least 5 minutes everyday.
3. What makes you happy? We had listed this down in one of the D-60 challenges. Go back to it and pick any one activity and DO IT on a daily basis.

If your answer to the 2nd question was the same, then I want you to do this: go back to D-15 and choose any one of the activities and do it on a daily basis.

If your answer to the 3rd question was the same, I want you to repeat the things we did on D-39 and do the exercise of D-38 everyday.

If your answer to the 4th question was the same, I want you to read what you wrote on D-18 once. Read D-17 after that. And starting from today, read what you had written on D-14 everyday.

If your answer to the 5th question was negative, do this:

1. Sit quietly with yourself
2. Ask why you didn't work on your goal today

3. Don't blame yourself, just ask the question and write down its answer.
4. Tell yourself this, say this out loud: What do I imagine myself doing after 10 years? Is it the me who has achieved my dreams? My goal/s? If not, then do I want to spend all these years in regret? No. It might not be for 10 hours daily, but for just 10 minutes, but I WILL work on my goal. I will stay consistent, so that in the future I get to enjoy the fruits of my hard work today.

If your answer to the 5th question was positive, I want you to maintain that consistently.

Lastly, the D-60 ends today. Thank you for being with me on this initiative. I hope I was of some help!

Congratulations on completing this initiative! I'm so so so proud of you!!

I just want one thing in return though. One promise from you:

Include some of these activities in your daily schedule. Even if you have done nothing, and even if you've scaled summits, no matter what happens, I want you to do this every day. Before going to bed, I want you to tell yourself this: "You did good today. I'm proud of you. Let's do good tomorrow."

www.ingramcontent.com/pod-product-compliance
Lightning Source LLC
Chambersburg PA
CBHW040736120726
48007CB00008B/110